for Tristan

Play Boogie

easy pieces in rock, jazz and pop style
for piano or electric keyboard by

DARYL RUNSWICK

FABER *ff* MUSIC

© 1989 by Faber Music Ltd
First published in 1989 by Faber Music Ltd
3 Queen Square London WC1N 3AU
Music drawn by New Notations
Cover illustration © Penny Dann 1989
Cover design by M & S Tucker
Printed in England

TO THE PUPIL

Do you wish you could play like your favourite group? Well now you can learn how! These pieces work just as well on electric keyboard or piano, and when you've finished this book you'll be on the way to being a great rock, jazz and pop keyboard player. Rock on!

TO THE TEACHER

Most children who learn the piano show a keen interest in trying to play rock, jazz and pop. The idea behind these books is to harness this enthusiasm to the ulterior motive of developing a good keyboard technique. The pieces are graded from easy to more difficult, following on from *Boogie for Beginners*, and can be introduced into a normal learning programme from time to time.

   Each piece develops aspects of rhythmic, melodic and chordal technique found in contemporary popular music. As pupils progress through the book they will find themselves acquiring hand-shapes and rhythmic patterns which they can use later in groups or as accompanists. In this respect the pieces are *Études*, using stock clichés to inculcate style, although I hope you will find them interesting and individual pieces of music in their own right.

PERFORMANCE NOTES

The pieces are written in the authentic notation used by the popular music professionals. This does not always seem the most logical notation to a classically-trained musician, but once certain things are pointed out it presents few problems. It would be foolish to adopt a seemingly more logical system that the pupil would have to 'unlearn' later:

1.   The player will find fewer phrase-slurs than might be expected in conventional piano music. Phrasing is nevertheless just as important here as elsewhere. It is not good style to play rock and jazz jerkily with no *legato*.

2.   The pieces are to be played in strict tempo except where a *rall* or *rit* is marked. This is especially true where the music seems to the classical musician to cry out for *rubato*. The main difference between classical and popular players' style is their attitudes to tempo – practice with a metronome (or even better a drum machine) is recommended.

3.   The sign > is used throughout in the popular music convention to show a syncopation and does not imply a big accent. The stress line (–) should be interpreted in the usual way.

4.   Those pieces using a jazz (*walking* or *swing*) beat use the notation ♩♩ for the swung melody. ♩³♪ is closer to what is actually played but is never used by professionals and therefore not here either.

DARYL RUNSWICK

Daryl Runswick
Play Boogie

Tornado Tris

Naturalie

Hunky Harry

26/7/95

*   *Tremolando*. It's like a *trill*, but the notes are not next to each other.

Shirley for Sure

NOTE: Rock and jazz pianists would play this piece in strict tempo – no *rubato*.

Slim Tim

Fair Helen

Stompin' Sam

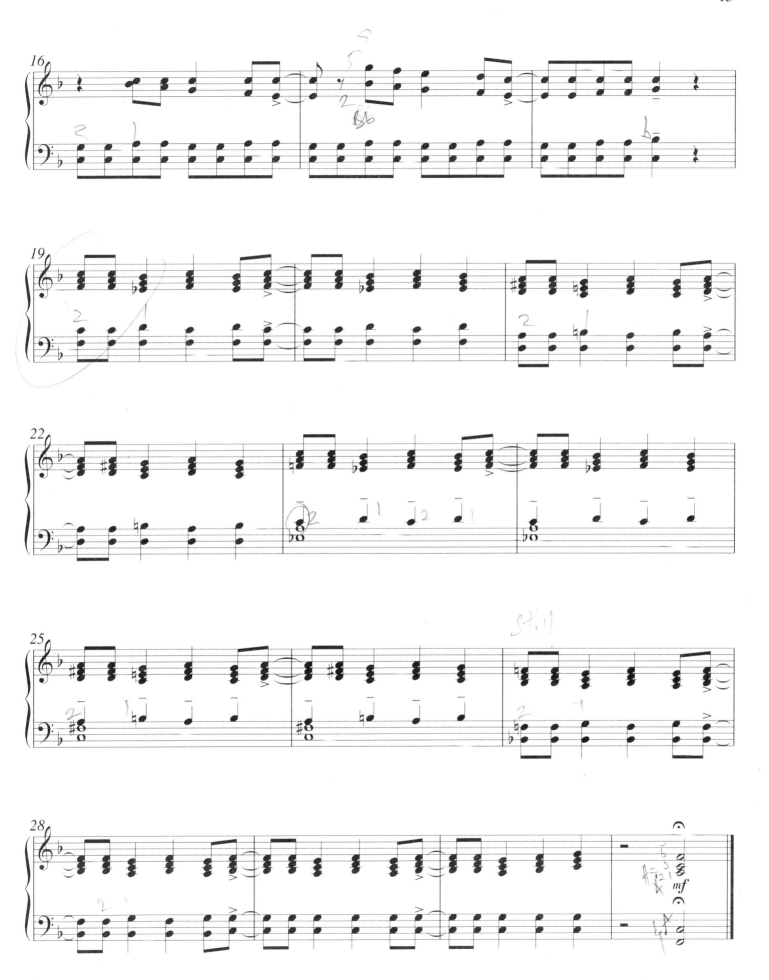

Funky Freda

17/7/96

* *Tremolando*. It's like a *trill*, but the notes are not next to each other.

Mungo's Mood

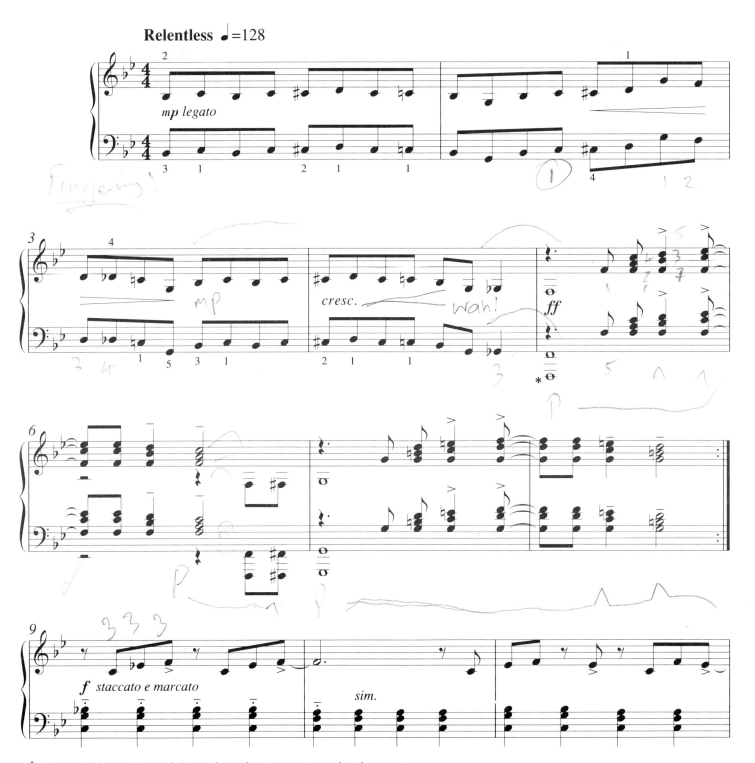

* If your keyboard doesn't have these bottom notes, miss them out.

Sharon Share-Alike

Winston Sebastian (duet)

SECONDO

NOTE: You can also play this as a solo piece in its own right.

Winston Sebastian (duet)

PRIMO

Maddy My Dear (duet)

SECONDO

Busy ♩=144

NOTE: You can also play this as a solo piece in its own right.

Maddy My Dear (duet)

PRIMO